JUNE

JUNE

FENCE
BOOKS

ALBANY · NEW YORK

daniel brenner

Published in the United States by Fence Books, Science Library 320, University at
Albany, 1400 Washington Avenue, Albany, NY 12222, www.fenceportal.org

Fence Books is a project of Fence Magazine, Incorporated, which is funded in
part by support from the New York State Council on the Arts and the National
Endowment for the Arts, along with the generous sponsorship of the New York
State Writers Institute and the University at Albany. Many thanks to these friends
and to all Friends of Fence.

Fence Books are distributed by Consortium Book Sales & Distribution (cbsd.com)
and printed in Canada by The Prolific Group (www.prolific.ca)

Design by Fence Books

Library of Congress Cataloguing in Publication Data
Brenner, Daniel [1976–]
June/ Daniel Brenner

Library of Congress Control Number: 2011922875

ISBN 13: 978-1-934200-43-8

FIRST EDITION
10 9 8 7 6 5 4 3 2

CONTENTS

Part two of national
Baronet
Let us think of times
We see orchids eaten
In a tincture hidden
By ice & pure
Topaz cinnamon sugar
Lettuce it's good 2
A mildewed radioactive
Orchid whip
Full of lintels
Arsenic & gardenias
Coal
Not all underwater
Palsied pioneers
A radioactive heat
Lies
The flood is coming
Time to wrap chemicals
About the whirlpool
With speciousness

CROWD

He lies here
Because of fertile
Seaside gardens
& klaxon
Sounds
Green & add
No dazzled salamanders

Whispers about
Photographs &
Chord changes
Too fast for questions
Another boat spins by
Piled high with herrings
& snake tongues

We're all about the whirlpool's
Flavors

June is coming
Let every city hear
Every umbrella
& every ant ear
Before the storm
Spend nights winging
Riddles at trees
About planting pioneers
This is a book
An ear
A throat
A city
Come bury it
Come loose
Get back

TRIANGULAR DUSK

Pioneers invaded
They climbed walls
On broken ladders trailing woven limbs
Looking at the rising water
Afraid of the storm
They depended on their helium pagodas

& floating on satiety
Islands
Night roads exquisite
Graves movies floods

The solar flares
Primordial ooze
Spooked animals
It'll rise
& scatter
The ice

Fungus of resentment
Can of dents
Whirlpool of ooze
Flood of Sno-Cones
Salamander paradise
Of war debris
To the edge of roads
& deep in
Admiration of the
Garden in love's
Cave with laughter &
Upside down
Hypocrisy
It's a doorway to paradise
Red & serrated
Deep in my solar plexus
The whirlpool is
An infinite vertical light beam

LEFTOVER SEQUINS

Delight for a week
Leftover sequins
Fire & heat of
Oozing mud
On floors squealing w/
Fire salamanders transplanted
To replace liquor leaders
Saying lock it away
& we went to a window
To be transplanted into
Fate
& huddled near jets

She emerged clean
And young with chapped skin
I imagine her food
Sacrifices to the leaders
Wings of innocence on her robotic face
Through a dazed blue mist
As she moves towards the sea
& more of life's awards

Before the flood he was
Smaller and hidden
Bugs ate
Let us consider it
Solemnly & strobe-lit
Through corridors
Howling for burial
In the churning earth of
Hillside rain
And glowing in five
Lineups
Let us dash food
Near the faces of dolphins
Thunderbolts from chemical
Faces on wings
The horse gallops and slows

FILTHY WELL

A witness to language
Founded by pioneers
With cordite on their faces &
I volunteer
To drift free past this plaster
I will get some sleep on the bus
When they discover underwater
Wear cloth shoes with the backs turned in
Fields of home
You put on candy
& more
My hands are so dirty
Flaked mud's strewn all over
The fire blazing
Unabashed arrivals
Agate snakes

Here was a question
A question of the stars
& here it is
Comet
Will your teeth
Fall on the bus
Burnt barded forelimbs
Flared goblins in acid clouds
Silver levitating horses

THRU TIN

Blunted outside of their wagons
Perfumed people inside were
Chewing gum
On bolts of silk
Protected by Xi An

She comes through cover
Smiling let us smile
& shine our sleeves with breath
Under a rainbow reflection

In this dimension
The cart's full of morphine
We can drool on the sky
In a state of completeness
Appointed sunlight

Or on a road marker
Somewhere the ghost & ice
It says here
Turn profane &
I turned & slid
Deep
With dirty hands
On green zinc roofs
Mud all over
Flaking in burning pine hot below
Hot as the arsonist's throat
They make us seep
From corners & in leeched gasps
We post marbles &
Drown our clones in fish tanks

Before the flood
A pioneer waited
With weapons
Under a white tent
A temporary sun flared
The soup was brass
Rocks bones & gunpowder
Were tamped

The flood came & took down
A wall of tape & bees
Body snatchers glowed
Like cabbages
As rapids bloomed
& veterans sifted the wash
For fish
A house is like a tent
A ticket is like two suns

Sure march back through
Black night blur in their black suits
Anymore do they
Older I say tut-tut
Radiation perfume

Chrome you know
Reflects green rays
It takes a lot less than 2
Days of vert until
The whirlpool melts ice
& people fall from their favorite seasons

Back before then trees leaned N she used to tell N
Through each burning Doppler drone
Green waves rotated
Around an island

There was nothing but sounds
& it was kind of hot
Wired gates snapped
15 of them
Through each burning embers
Of pine spread across the gravel

HORSE

He loved to win
As anvils banged
Gleaming grime
She sells storms
Anvil beats
Labeled this & that
Losing touch
Loop level gesture
Look up
Please
Slips
Into snowy mist
It's important
Alloy chemical aliens &
Contortionist ices
Yes war & paintings of railroads
Skids
Anvils
War-words
Anvils
Virtue
Anvils
Several plants
Including
Sunflowers
&
Meanwhile in distant cars
The scrawl is maybe deciphered

Chewing her right-flavor gum
Flashbacks ensue in which
A nest of figures burns &
Mud around them boils
Their feet are buried in after-boil
& strewn with water
It's fine
As hot mud dries & flakes
On the hardwood floor
The stars spin
21cm

How clean her teeth
How tender at her nest
Of animals
So similar
What a damaging fire

GOLDEN

Xi An is a guardian of paradise
She protects the pioneer children
Of pearly handbags
With net & trident

She came through a long frost
& after weeks of dredging mud
We saw her from the island
As the trash washed by

Something tumbles
& your young swirl
Free as birds

There is no cape
There is no nebula
There is no island

THE DAZE

Body snatchers
Have stolen Xi An's child
From the garden
During the storm
In a flash of water
People have all struggled
With the war
The whirlpool is strident
In its savagery
Its storm

Mine
I have a mic
Held up to the sea breeze
Let us harvest the poison
Dazzled & jealous
Of the people on their island
They are like lynxes
They know better

FAKE ART SODA

Before the flood
Hit the development company
We all lived in condos
Like responsible adolescents
Harvesting rumors
& making art soda
With no narrative
Except one kid
Who got the funnies

Our characters
Weren't developed
I haven't tried it yet
Our wings locked on the mountain
So that our art soda
Would taste like soup
It helped us keep our cool

A girl stands
Drinking from her mitten
In front of a young tree
She goes towards upside down
Pale yellow & blue
Where seas warp in edges
Like flaxen saucers
Keep talking too fast
Shaking in broken
Swoops & angles
Throwing stuff
It's raining again
Dripping trees
Primordial backwash
Underneath all the liquor
It's independence day
At the Hotel Photinia
Paradise flycatchers
& tigers

They were given pallets
For blistering synthesis
Jellyfish
Before the bees drowned
& filled statues
Fearlessly
I awaited malfunction
Completely politely
Wearing suitable clothing
With salamander hands
& the way horses go
Outdoors after rain with
Luxurious apple cravings

We will sacrifice questions like
Is it the same
To radiation's light
With love's air anguish
You know where
Gorgeous dolphins will thrash &

Radioactive wagons burn
Dollops of cinnamon sugar
Will flow in jets 2 vases
They will flee as the waters surge

The books will float awhile
Away from their private heat
Of TVs & space stations
Hot light will tramp down traces &
Tumble handfuls of camouflage
Into the cover where they will wait for you

The egrets
I mean
The radioactive shack will be gone
Its concrete will have tumbled
Under a chorus of storms

Virtue's sting escaped the storm
Well it's high noon
Virtue's second dirty hollow is to the left
Well people can park there
A series of heart-shaped mirrors

It's full of chemicals
To encapsulate shelves
Our pens & whip handlers
Drive the mustached pioneers through the war
They cry the way it was

Gold she draws my eyes closed
She is carrying all of you
Here is an entry
It's one of the radioactive houses remember
All opposite
Everything is backwards
A complete window harvest
Delight in virtue's lash

COMET

Before the storm
There was a workshop on floods
I slept through class so I missed
The slithering doctor's lecture about how
Beautiful they were

Pioneers died with cordite
In their mustaches
The backwash below
Rose to consume them
Whirlpool wait

Whirlpool devastate
The pioneers
Feed them as snails
Might as well break it all down

We know what caused the flood
But we forgot
We know how life began
It was with birds flying through
We know how the harvest was done
It was with hot water
We know what the floor looks like
Hot and flaky mud is everywhere
We laugh in our sleep
About the arsonist now
It's sad
That the gate's chained

Ticking against the remaining concrete
A compass has flipped on the dashboard
In similar news
The statues bubble with snowmelt
& pioneers float
As mud flows
& five wise voices
Express their indifference
Along the confluence

I was there by the pier
Wearing rotten clothes
Making a statue that
Kept falling over
Somehow I got here
To where the reeds are

The body snatchers are
Still underground
She meant that their clothes
Were filthy too
As I swam through paradise
Above the fields

She sounded sweet like
A girl who talks about green rays
& snakes while tapping a stick
On the ground & stirring
Salamanders
In the mud
To
Marvelous
Underwater
Calm
Music

FLOOD

I was just a shell by then
X flashed in the rearview
I tried to outrun it w/whiskey
The stairs are no good anymore

Second floor cats
Ruby how are they doing
Do you have a dove spoon
Where is the gate by the way
Sheer depth & waves

This is where pink cat insides
Drink w/ Ruby Horse
& move into gallons
For art in the night

He is there too with code
I was driving that car Jim talked about
& doing light tricks looking out windows
They make everything a mystery
Relative to what was what was
Written on the van
& which still when the clock switch ticks
Against war jails
Sits there on the side of the van
Pay attention to the flashlight beam
I don't know where
Put it on the floor
Lose that idea about
What is immanent
& fight your way back to sleep

DIRTY RIBBON

Sir Wooly Mammoth
& some of his friends
Knocked up against ooze bags
They are going to stop the flood
& avert all disaster
In the cloud shrine
They are going to take the train

The mud is so hot & dry
It flakes from my feet
Squid
& Flute
Get off my balcony
Oh I'm so sure
I stand beside the river
Don't ask me
Who's going to win

BITTER

Seven lion tamer girls smear blood
On their teeth as the whirlpool's agents
Fire arrows at wagons

Outside crickets chirp
The whiz of the storm & blood flow
On Blood Show St.
Where wagons full of liquor
Stop there underwater
The ruins of arcades
War
& pixels
The sun sets
On an aquamarine lion

The whirlpool controls 2 doors
With red writing
It is big enough to stand again
Breaking off in spiral ice particles
Regarding that
The whirlpool tells us stars
Wrong among stars are so we think
Up there on the ceiling
Slides
Iced out in a solar flare
Sky and bird satellite crash
& feet flake mud on the floor
Transportation & hedges
Tropes & secrets

ENDURANCE

Xi An's child
Washed away in the flood
Wagons scattered N and E
The broken compass doomed us
& dogs gathered
Down on forgotten avenues
With crumbling medieval detainees
Swimming in greed
Cursing
I am in a light boat
Sheathed in primordial ooze

The thaw brings storm
Winds & marquees
Candy they seem to lean
Sacrificial war meat
Such clever little teeth
Behind machines
Fidgeting
Her benevolence is as crooked
As mine is
Central air
Sings her song
The offering
A levitant's feast of motes

RADIOACTIVE

I am just
Barely
The room
Dateline
Body snatchers have called
Whirlpool
& my heart is
A red slip cover
A team they say
Captain
Get in the white building

The whirlpool handle is 5
Open handle is gone
Librium
Fire
Let's take a breath

It's not for stolen pioneers
Broken & burnt
Their cities underwater first
Their children clinging to reeds
Stealing our ideas
War
Corpses in the snow

The sun has roused the
Animals inside of us
& dashed the satellites to pieces
Things like good N evil
Are irrelevant
The body snatchers
Tepidly rise from hardwood floors
What if I say
3 of them

STEAM

I am following the flood
In my car
Take me to that green place again
Where the Pegasus has bottle caps
& Xi An's got the morphine
Thank you my absorbers
There is nothing to forgive
Here is that paradise
It made you so frustrated
Thank you for paradise
Mr. Reason owns the vaporized owl-track
Out in the desert that is ½ circus
Those who line up in front may
Absorb OK

O

Always ready
You loyal class
Descendants of pioneers
You have saved a lot of ice

A large phone is right
On shadowy wings
About charming storms
Crossing the earth

That dull sine
S AM rain
Covered in grease &
Birds

All skied & muddy
It's a book though
But not really
Yup 21 cm
Beam it out

Help us hold on
See the smoke from
Our wagons
See our flag waving

Pure evil western demons
She can burn them silently
She is preparing explosives
To test out in the forest
As long as we protect her
There will be no fires

There is a sack of primordial ooze
Beneath their intentions
All the king's radioactive gate
Mushroom heads are
Lazy
Like typical furniture
Studiousness
Cold & a gate of black sheathed hulls in breeze
Long singing for floor cleaning
My arm
My king
My ace
The storm

Birds wheel above
In storm winds in droves
Salamanders of the mud
Drs and firemen
Of the sun

The whirlpool divines
Sacrifice
The arsonist is poisoned
Burnt
The colors fall off
Chains of sanity
Scores of puppies
Telephones
The sun is at war
Throwing off its solar flares
Making all the animals cower
& shiver

CHARGE

An invasive rocket shot up
From the poison desert
Thanks
Finally
From a steel TV war garden
Where they wear
The latest masks
Let us recede into the ooze
Screen our storm machines
What does it matter
Whether or not to leave one
For history
Until we are again hungry
To dance with the barber
& her woolen handbag

We made rockets &
The future is made of meditations on
Hunger
Beauty & thirst
I am as one in a doomed charge

HOT SPEECH

Snacks
White sand beaches
Pariah dogs
Bitter medieval profanity
Crow tracks

The deep pioneers there had their
Cloth on display
& we blew up w/them
In an 80 degree garden looking
I mean loving hu-hu
Z was it in
The X-spot air
Reversal
Or something more automatic
Turn around

Her music wasn't that territorial
Here are the keys to our car
They shine next to her secret heart
It is OK here with the dolphins
Whirlpool woo fast cars catfish

I mean it doesn't matter anymore
We are on the team with
Masks

Flood
& strangling fodder
Comfortable about what
Full pioneers' children
Put up in the dead heat
There was something not

Exactly my screen is for
Catching rain in divisions
& including hands from fake windows
With building switches turned over silver
Tilting it into cloth sacks
When they say nothing
In unison before soft

Admit it to yourself
You're thinking still
In like 10 chemical keys
Used to put to question
Big elements C right star
Did U see that heat when
The student whirlpool's agents invaded
& burned the 10 sacrificial wagons

Evil blood I know you are the
Night we put under·
To light our wet windows
To advertise our heat
Mud flakes on the hardwood
Whiskey floor title reversal
Whirlpool window war animals
Hot rivers swollen
With rain

We take blistered photography
A ruined choice buried under
Muddy roads
How about a biscuit snowflake

How about a wall of flowers
Trees are free to go
Into rain & start chemical
Training on trains
To lean

When it gets warm
Bringing a new day
Drama
In Mark's chemical divining booth

LIGHT

Skulls of the bored
Love in English
It went up like cream
In a fake oasis & I am

Behind this lacquered spotlight
Shining on jade
& rainbow whirlpools
Recast in our levitant harvests

That morning we drank tea
From the skull of the mushroom princess
Like lambs

& blessed the clothing of warring states
Because when they are damp
& graze 21cm away
They will wheel into necessary rising waters
Looking for our evil wagon
Burning faces flash by
In places

ASHTRAY

Deserts are where there are roots
Dispel non rock floor students
Pushing on love for farfetched
Schemes in deserts green
From the king & war in green since
I don't consider it red
And let all the king's green seep into it
That's why people who live there
Take on the grail again since it was on
Water the second time that things started to
Really they could really happen
Sometime
& that one time before
Flight I'm in the building
Her mother is up in there too

HOROSCOPE

Caryatids saluting royalty
Lit up all nice and fake
Like they're pure evil

The distant whirlpool
From slow thaws
A storm takes a car
Into striated levels of water
I sit in the rain with nuns

They grow weaker
Unprepared
Balladic leaves hide their faces
Justice swings on a silver chain
The reaper arrives for them on stilts
Of Styrofoam
Strung with fishnets

Muddy fish breathe suspended there
Just like we'll be able to

IN SUNLIGHT

The wrong telephone rang
& they waved hissing salt shakers
Hello guy it's like I said before
Stretch you loved it on our island

8 chemical shores
Then war
It makes more sense that there was
Some kind of gate to edgy knowledge methods
Around something real close
It is all right pushing war

The pagoda's song of death
Courage said it all in numbers
Bright
Braided
Sunlight

Fur gates
N
Ssh
Who remembers
I'm sleepy
Greenstick stupor
Poems lilting whirlpool
60 m away
Xi An is at the apex
For work the whirlpool's agents
Dressed all like soldiers
Killed all pioneer
Stock & left behind ruins
If you look in B tube it says
Snakes

JUNGLE

She has a pretty face
As she sits twisting her
Stuffed lion
Dippy sweaty noon
Times where crayons
Cross mud blistered
Stars of small hells

There beyond is a solitary
Pioneer lazily hacking at cabbage
Let us think of his roots
His sanitary pearly home
A treasure
Grab your medieval handbag
Your woolen hunger
Sidestep everything else

The whirlpool is full of
Lion music
Children of pioneers
Have managed to weave
Jade gifts into it
That aren't even remembered
Decks will contain anything
Oars movies N
My soda next to yours
Morphine leaks from the edges
Of the rings they condense
Fluorescent prophecies

Dead everywhere
War
Wanton butchery
I invite you
In angry storms
On the banks of rivers
Crumbling amidst
Balloons flecks of
Chemicals
Will June never come
Has June come already
When the rainbow shines
Guttural fortune tellers
Promise heavenly love
Amidst the shame & slaughter
A rainbow of birds
Levitation & tobacco
Music has already fucked this
Some hate the loyalty implied
We gaze at the mountain anyway
Contemplating how good the soup was

TREASURE

Ain't no telephone
In a blood of a world in my war
They at a dolphin has
What I need the

Ice going by fast
It's the same thing every day
On are we an island
There thin man hands me at cloth

Half bird
It ain't no same green black
Her hair changed
The lion did whatever it wanted like

Despite X fact that water was great
I was sick signed
Love was too heavy
It was time for something else

GARDEN

It is not green
It's where we wait
For crooked hooks to rain
& the running last section to
Hiss with wires

It's been used up
About time
The storm champion
Crossed chalk lines
Wet mattresses
Drunk old boys
Square-o
Keep going S
Choose the red crutch

CORRECT

Virtuously virtue's telephone agrees with me
Like a noise that brings me to my darkened boat
Mud is spattered along the port hull
& I have swum through the demon halls
Understanding it
Planning my next cat
As I reach the island
It is like a movie
In which I'm trapped & alive
Scrambling to a cord or raft or wicked wrath
The malfunction is all sort of lost

In the wilderness & you find it and understand &
Bring it in to give it a haircut
Or bob its tail
Of course this is put out
By educated people
Who know how to work at anvils
Even when they're fucked up
Their islands are beautiful
Walled in rippling silver screens
The ground is so soft there

Xi An I am flying a kite
Out in the locusts
Xi An I am locking riddles
In the tiny concrete beehive
Before the flood it was raining
I am suffering waiting
I will go through the entryway
& speak of nothing among
The floating ashtrays
& empty pill bottles
Let those who bite their nurses
Reflect on moon/water
Go ahead & steal from
The hot smoking wet mortar craters
A handful of this hot mud
She is blind now
The arsonist
I will make a place where
We are all blind
The sea is inside out
& our muddy hands
Are also stained with arsenic
Xi An I'm the guy who pretended
I was a pioneer
I wear a strange cape now

SACRIFICE

The storm that stirs the
Whirlpool is a tyrant
Living in a great golden hall
Everyone is exhausted
Everyone is in love
Everyone is pregnant
Let us think
Everyone is drunk
The tyrant sucks it down like wisdom like a parasite
From subjects
Which are pondered amidst his magic cabinets

LIQUOR

Um look at the paper
Scratch head
I don't know
Su
Is this the flood part
A horse inhales
Outrageous storms
I consider storms beautiful
Outside
Um
Tap pen or something
They all hatched
Repeat
Near the gate
Winter gate
Bright and shining
Xi An
I also see the cold moon in the water

Pure evil
Lights go out
Your savior robbed
We remember when
They made balanced music
About it

In the plutonium dark
I can take their used balladic weapons from tall buildings
& cut through filthy walls
To get to it

Let us think of good N evil
& remind ourselves

That we are victims
Of a constant forgetfulness

My inkblot looks like
We were just leaving
A moldy funhouse
Nothing but a mistake
Before we play pool & iron we are ghosts
Of ourselves now & then
Drinking
We are liars
& thieves too

DICTATOR

Ice flows by in moist washes
Except in the greases
Styrofoam & clothes
The flood
Birds like hunks of rock

It is the whirlpool's fault
Farfetched violins
Xi An is there &
What about the windows

Divine justice
Is a morphine a mirror
Is a mushroom a pioneer
Does an evil please baby

After wool
Lunch remains
Wise alligators
Climb old trees
& finally the music seems to agree

Whistling down roads
The ghosts of birth's rain roam
Bleakly
Expensively too
& she says
Something that rhymes with cruel
It's cheaper than this
Shopping along for art's sake

New teams approach
All familiar
They count their steps in lobbies loud
& steel their sleeping supplies
In war-torn skies
Moving like ice on high floes
Of Styrofoam all summer
These kids and their capes

A TRIP TO THE ISLAND

The island is like
A nun's hug
In a black car
On the island
In afterimages
Forever

Retinal
Aftertastes
Bring candy
2 radioactive reeds
Books
Burn or are buried

Like the sun makes a deer
Nervous upstream
Amidst mountain ice
From spring
Stumbling along islands
& lying

Xi An inhales
Doppler is in style
Throaty lovels
Shoes off for this part
Fast food
It's an old saw

Forever with underground tunnels
Multidimensional separation
Tarnished & free
Like a vaporized owl
Lying
About
In the primordial ooze

Burned
Full of eunuchs
Horses & whistles
Sunshine through
Cornstalks
An appetite of style
Old songs
Morphine

Call a taxi
I do generate
Beauty & filth
Follow the smoke
& slime
To the hill
Of ooze
She is gone
Free of nightlight cheese
Burning behind her
Her remaining contributions
Like flecks of puke
On the dashboard

The eunuchs said
Before the war
It is mostly beauty & goodness
Lovely food
Surrounded by wheeling birds
The levitants

She listened to the eunuchs
Butchered a motorcycle engine lock post &
Turned the key
She's free

A diseased pioneer breaches
Into her primordial ooze
In the halls of beauty & goodness
& the hammered caves of desire

Xi An is here to mark a copy
Full of containers
Tap an eraser against her teeth
Visit the bees
&

War
No more lies
Fill our 1 vase left

You will sleep through this
& awaken with a cry
To an old wise blanket
& a stern winter storm
While the urge to be consists
Of a daze of criminality
Which must be snappier
Each year
Through the magic of alchemists
Mystics & Floridians
Of oil pans & hamburgers
In streets of lettuce
Note sometimes we will substitute
Cabbage
Marching o'er
Behind where the 10th beach brigade
Crossed with orange dividers
The crow-strewn snowfall

Her lyrics are covered
As a boat pulls up
I am on the boat with Xi An
She talked about the dogs
& a bunch of meat-skins
& whistled thru her decaying teeth
Like a cricket
Like a Loa her leg moved to the music
& bone shades with sharkskin shone
Neon blue
In the filthy cold sea

SHE

She knows how to cut
Lettuce with a wine knife
She shakes around bright trees
Expensively
Heart attacks next to silk
The ribs R like chrome
They breathe themselves
Jail toes
Expanding dripping statements
Addicted to the petting zoo
Love tells me
What to do
Ever since
On gravel roadsides
Who
Who pagan
Mouth child
You dripping chrome vat
You chintz countered
Glimmer garden
In your locked
Silken
East

I love rain
I welcome war
Stare at the floor
Everything is backwards

Phones we tremble
Your ears at once
Shakes & sackcloth
It means you in a
Riddle light

This is the part she fears
I fear the whirlpool
That stirs up the original
& shoots all five flavors
Multidimensionally

Out in the distributing storm
Winter umbrellas
Onscreen flowers bloom

In the flood's wake
Myths drench
& defuse us

BUGS

PS silver rainbow pioneers
Are a pestilence
I can't see past the van
What did it say
Echo
The echo stays tough
Being gravity
I am driving & wear
Art
Near a big lake
Where the radio got it
First again

Fence Books has a mission to redefine the terms of accessibility by publishing challenging writing distinguished by idiosyncrasy and intelligence rather than by allegiance with camps, schools, or cliques. It is part of our press's mission to support writers who might otherwise have difficulty being recognized because their work doesn't answer to either the mainstream or to recognizable modes of experimentation.

The Motherwell Prize is an annual series that offers publication of a first or second book of poems by a woman, as well as a five thousand dollar cash prize.

The Fence Modern Poets Series is open to manuscripts by poets of any gender and at any stage of career, and offers a one thousand dollar cash prize in addition to publication.

For more information about either prize, or more information about *Fence*, visit www.fenceportal.org.

THE MOTHERWELL PRIZE

Negro League Baseball	Harmony Holiday
living must bury	Josie Sigler
Aim Straight at the Fountain and Press Vaporize	Elizabeth Marie Young
Unspoiled Air	Kaisȧ Ullsvik Miller

THE ALBERTA PRIZE

The Cow	Ariana Reines
Practice, Restraint	Laura Sims
A Magic Book	Sasha Steensen
Sky Girl	Rosemary Griggs
The Real Moon of Poetry and Other Poems	Tina Brown Celona
Zirconia	Chelsey Minnis

FENCE MODERN POETS SERIES

Nick Demske	Nick Demske
Duties of an English Foreign Secretary	Macgregor Card
Star in the Eye	James Shea
Structure of the Embryonic Rat Brain	Christopher Janke
The Stupefying Flashbulbs	Daniel Brenner
Povel	Geraldine Kim
The Opening Question	Prageeta Sharma
Apprehend	Elizabeth Robinson
The Red Bird	Joyelle McSweeney

NATIONAL POETRY SERIES

The Network	Jena Osman
The Black Automaton	Douglas Kearney
Collapsible Poetics Theater	Rodrigo Toscano

ANTHOLOGIES & CRITICAL WORKS

Not for Mothers Only: Contemporary Poets on Child-Getting & Child-Rearing
Catherine Wagner & Rebecca Wolff, editors

A Best of Fence: *The First Nine Years,* Volumes 1 & 2
Rebecca Wolff and *Fence* Editors, editors

POETRY

June	Daniel Brenner
English Fragments A Brief History of the Soul	Martin Corless-Smith
The Sore Throat & Other Poems	Aaron Kunin
Dead Ahead	Ben Doller
My New Job	Catherine Wagner
Stranger	Laura Sims
The Method	Sasha Steensen
The Orphan & Its Relations	Elizabeth Robinson
Site Acquisition	Brian Young
Rogue Hemlocks	Carl Martin
19 Names for Our Band	Jibade-Khalil Huffman
Infamous Landscapes	Prageeta Sharma
Bad Bad	Chelsey Minnis
Snip Snip!	Tina Brown Celona
Yes, Master	Michael Earl Craig
Swallows	Martin Corless-Smith
Folding Ruler Star	Aaron Kunin
The Commandrine & Other Poems	Joyelle McSweeney
Macular Hole	Catherine Wagner
Nota	Martin Corless-Smith
Father of Noise	Anthony McCann
Can You Relax in My House	Michael Earl Craig
Miss America	Catherine Wagner

FICTION

Prayer and Parable: Stories	Paul Maliszewski
Flet: A Novel	Joyelle McSweeney
The Mandarin	Aaron Kunin